USER FRIENDLY

BY ILLIAD

O'REILLY®

Beijing · Cambridge · Farnham · Köln · Paris · Sebastopol · Taipei · Tokyo

User Friendly
by Illiad

Printed in the United States of America.

Editor: Simon Hayes
Production Editor: Madeleine Newell

Printing History:
September 1999: First Edition

ISBN: 1-56592-673-0
[M]

[1/00]

To my parents,
for always guiding me to the fork in the road,
and then letting me choose which path to take.

The comic strips you are about to read are true. Only the names have been changed to protect the innocent . . .

At least, that's the way *User Friendly* reads sometimes. Like all good myths, it has elements that are a bit implausible. But like all good myths, we look in the mirror and see ourselves. Well . . . we do if we're Internet geeks, anyway.

Yes, it is a rare breed *User Friendly* celebrates—the happy few who have given up distractions like worldly success, social lives, and (much of the time) sleep, in order to pursue the *really* important things. Like the latest computer game. Or the perfect hack, evolved in jewel-like splendor at 3 A.M. in the morning. Or keeping the Internet running.

And if they look a bit ridiculous, that's OK. Without monomaniacs like these, who knows where the sane and boring rest of humanity would be? Their Pleistocene ancestors probably stayed up all night chipping flints in new patterns just to see the firelight gleaming off the facets; without them, we'd still be trying to get the hang of stone tools—and failing.

But I didn't come here today to write a panegyric to techno-nerds and hackers. I came to talk about their style of humor. It's edgy, surreal, brainy, gently self-mocking, but fundamentally kindhearted. It is intelligence without either apology or condescension; it's satire without superiority or irony or exhaustion. It combines passion for one's craft with a healthy refusal to get stuffy or self-important about same.

You can immerse yourself in this style of humor on USENET's *rec.humor.funny* group; you can learn about it in the Jargon File; you can hear it, if you listen carefully, almost any time hackers and techies get together to talk shop. Illiad has it down perfectly.

Other cartoonists ranging from Scott Adams to (even) Garry Trudeau have visited this space occasionally. Illiad lives there; he's part of the culture he's describing. His characters are undeniably authentic, drawn from life. And he's made them topical—his comics combine geek in-jokes with today's headlines.

So welcome to the wacked-out world of Columbia Internet. Because the real world is every bit as bizarre as this . . .

Eric S. Raymond
11 May 1999

ACKNOWLEDGMENTS

I have so many people to thank that I don't know where to begin; I also apologize in advance if I inadvertently forget to mention someone.

My thanks to:

Barry, Martina, and Beaner, the triumvirate of business sense that has kept me out of the soup kitchens.

Steven, Rob, Tom, Toomas, Heidi, Toni, Ken, and Pauline for inspiring me. Brad and Josette, for doing such a grand job with the UF merchandise.

Iambe, for her daily column, daily support, and valued friendship. Arcterex, for organizing *ufies.org*, being a great pal, and for promising never to wear a thong in my presence.

Dana, for being so giving with his support and friendship.

Ciannait, Kethryvis, Dire Wolf, Tricia, Thyla, Godmoma, Shorti, Belgand, Ritalin-Boy, and Latheos for helping me with the site and for just being pals.

Sillz, for her weekly column, her friendship, and for speaking Strine.

Eric, for his eloquent praise and support, and for representing the Open Source movement with heart.

David, for being such a cool literary agent and for securing the deal with O'Reilly & Associates.

Kirk, for believing in me and *User Friendly* enough to run us in Canada's most cutting-edge national newspaper.

Simon, for proving wrong in a spectacular way the myth that all book editors are evil pond scum who wear leather hoods and carry whips with authors' names inscribed on the grip.

Chris and Trae at VA Linux Systems for backing *User Friendly* just because they thought we were cool.

Alicia, Edie, and Rob at O'Reilly, the production people who always seem to remain unsung heroes for all of their hard work and drive.

UFies everywhere, without whom *User Friendly* would never have been successful.

And last but most certainly not least, Heather, for without her help, love, and support, I would not have believed in myself enough to even try.

COLOPHON

The cover images for *User Friendly* were designed by Illiad. Kathleen Wilson designed and produced the cover layout using QuarkXPress 3.3. Alicia Cech designed and produced the interior layout using QuarkXPress 3.3, the Monotype Gill Sans font, and the Comics CarToon font. Madeleine Newell was the production editor. The images in the book were prepared for print by Robert Romano and Rhon Porter using Adobe Photoshop 5.

Many fans have asked me to explain how I started on the strip, and others want to know where I get my ideas from.

I'm not entirely certain what motivated me to pick up that pen and start scrawling the first *User Friendly* cartoon at work. I had been watching and participating in the office antics for years, and had never before felt any urge whatsoever to draw pictures of my coworkers in compromising positions. Suddenly, it just seemed to be the thing to do, and away I went. All of the characters fell into place, because they all existed in real life. The dynamics were there, the personalities were obvious, and all of a sudden I had a full-blown cast.

The stories and jokes came readily. We were a happy bunch playing games like Quake in the office those days anyway, so I found the humor right in front of my face. Stef's complaints about Greg's priorities vaguely mirror what happened in reality, and Stef's conversion to playing Quake also took place for real. Of course, not all of what has developed in *User Friendly* is exactly based on reality; I felt I had to inject some creativity into it to justify my involvement.

For instance, Pitr's real-life analog actually has an Estonian heritage (Estonian isn't at all Slavic, it's closest to Finnish), but the blatantly fake Slavic accent affected by Pitr was too campy to pass up. The Smiling Man's analog doesn't really smile all day, he just smiles when he wants to get your panties in a knot. And Erwin and the Dust Puppy . . . well, I won't get into how much reality is involved with them, for reasons of national security.

I had originally drawn the Dust Puppy in the late 70s, when I was just a kid. In the mid-80s, I actually drew about two dozen cartoons for a strip that I simply called "Dust Puppies," which was about an eight-year-old boy named Timmy and the strange fuzzy creature born from the dust balls under his bed. I submitted my cartoons to about half a dozen syndicates, and of course all I got back were rejection slips. I shelved the cartoons and resigned myself to a life of corporate servitude.

It's now more than a decade later, and here I am with my first book and a huge audience of fans without the help of the syndicates. And all of it came from some strange conceptual seed in my head that decided to sprout at that particular moment.

Many people consider the seed from which ideas spring to be a rare and valuable item. I suppose at some level it is, but for the most part, I believe ideas come easily—it's their execution (in terms of time, equity, money, or effort) that is the hard part.

Someone once told me that working as a cartoonist must be a really cushy gig. "Draw funny pictures all day? You have it easy." I took the time to explain that what was involved was a production deadline once a day, every day, 365 days a year. He gave me a glassy-eyed stare, then started laughing. "Man, it sucks to be you."

But you know, I'm not complaining! Doing this cartoon strip is immensely rewarding and tons of fun. I take great pleasure in making people laugh, from quiet smiles to hysterical screaming belly howls. Taking jabs at large, arrogant corporations and idiotic governments also has its own rewards. But the best payback, the one that has emerged out of left field and ambushed me, is the tremendous support of a very large and very loyal community.

This community is, thanks to the Internet, truly global. For example, there are regular readers in Israel, Brazil, Iceland, New Zealand, Romania, Qatar, and Greece, to name just a few. At one point, the site was getting several daily hits from Antarctica! One of the most rewarding aspects is the number of different kinds of people who seem drawn to the strip—everybody from an 81 year-old woman ("Finally, something on the Internet I can relate to!") to a nine year-old girl ("Dear Mr. Illiad, please send me a real-life Dust Puppy. Thank you.").

Ultimately, it's comments like the ones above that make drawing *User Friendly* so worthwhile. One letter I get over and over goes something like: "Illiad, thanks for the cartoons. You make me smile on Monday mornings." I've received thousands of versions of that sentiment, and I never get tired of reading them.

Making people smile is the greatest reward I could ever have—and I want to thank you all for your letters, for reading my book, and for laughing at my drawings.

USER FRIENDLY
by
Illiad

tappity
tappity
tappity

Hey little guy.
What're you
doing?

I'm experimenting with this
artificial intelligence I
just developed.

Hello A.J. Want to
see a design I've
been working on?

YE GODS! This is
incredible!

STEF! PUT YOUR
MARKETING
HAT ON!

What's with him?

I think he's just
impressed that I
can type with my toes.

I'm telling you Stef, the dust puppy
created an artificial intelligence. It's
uncanny. Look at those weird patterns
on the screen.

You're right. I wonder what those patterns mean.
Maybe it's a code, or a visual representation of
flowing intelligence. Maybe it's what the philosophers
have been looking for all these years.

Actually, it's
my screen saver.

1

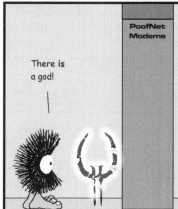

16

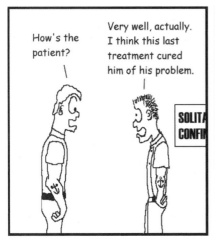

21

You reading that stuff on Leo Hindery's remarks about the Internet presenting a great threat to decency and morality?

Yeah, what an idiot.

Maybe, but he's got the Roman Catholic Church backing him.

Makes you wonder how a cable executive can get that kind of support.

Hey Guiseppe! Isn't that Jenny McCarthy?

And today on the Playboy Channel...

Hey, you seen Pitr around today?

He went to see the doctor. Something about X-rays.

Is it serious?

Not sure. Pitr's been complaining about chest pains for the past few weeks.

That is the most remarkable chest film I've ever seen. You have two hands inside of you.

I think I'm going to hurl.

anatomy of a crud puppy

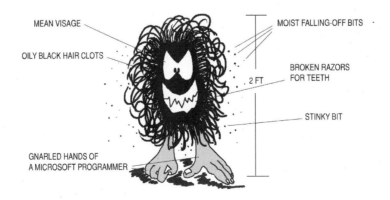

MEAN VISAGE

OILY BLACK HAIR CLOTS

MOIST FALLING-OFF BITS

BROKEN RAZORS FOR TEETH

2 FT

STINKY BIT

GNARLED HANDS OF A MICROSOFT PROGRAMMER

23

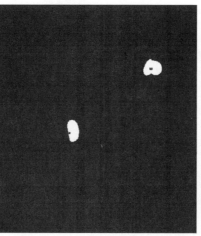

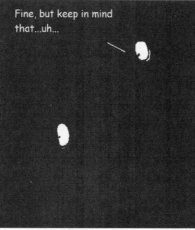

27

My, that looks terribly anti-social. What is that?

Quake.

Never heard of it. Perhaps you can explain it to me.

And then I told him it was a new video-conferencing tool and that I was controlling a cybernetic killer to hunt down an executive of a company I used to work for.

Oh God, STOP!

Hello Mr. CEO. Are you here to help elevate the common high-tech worker to unbounded levels of productivity, or are you just an executive hack?

It's a valid ethical question.

Why am I talking to a toilet brush?

Ed Mustecki, a Year 2000 expert, was interviewed today on the catasrophic results that computer systems will suffer at the end of the millenium.

When asked about the photographs of Bill Gates and Saddam Hussein that were pinned to his wall, Ed remarked, "They both vindicate the Year 2000 issue."

When asked what he meant by that statement, Mr. Mustecki replied, "It just goes to show, civilized countries can be potentially brought to their knees by a couple of zeroes."

Columbia Internet Technical Support. Greg speaking, how may I help you?

I have a problem.

We all do, buddy. Deal with it.

Greg speaking. May I help you?

Hi. Uh. Yeah. Got a problem with Windows 95.

TAP TAP TAP

Story of my life. What's the problem?

It's not recognizing his modem. I mean, my modem.

"His" modem? Who's modem are we talking about?

My modem! Definitely my modem!

iCan't Internet — Tech Support Department

Who is this anyways?!

I think we've been made.

Then call the customer back and tell him we need more time!

I was just comparing the speed of our Web server to that of iCan't Internet's. We were faster for a while, but for some reason we've slowed way down.

That does seem rather strange. There must be something very intensive running on our Web server. I'll ask one of the techs.

Ah, how fortuitous. Greg, I wanted to ask you...

Would you mind not using our Web server? We're trying to have a game of Quake here.

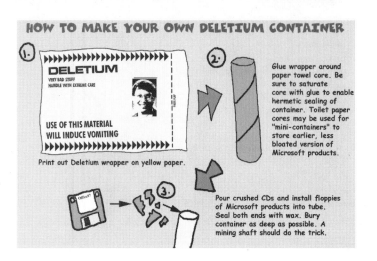

USER FRIENDLY
by
Illiad

There's Microsoft headquarters. Looks clear. Go for it, little dude.

Okay.

Um, what precisely am I going to do with Microsoft HQ?

If I could answer that I'd be working for the DOJ.

USER FRIENDLY
the comic strip

Portrasher 4

ROTO-ROUTER 800

Well it's about time you SWAT guys got here! We've got Gates and his boys cornered in a boardroom. Better bring up your heavy weapons.

Wasn't that a DOJ agent?

Yes. And it looks like we get to assault a boardroom full of vice-presidents with two geeks and a puffball.

Mr. Gates, this is your last chance. The SWAT team is here. Come out peacefully and we won't be forced to use extreme measures.

NEVER! We have a great Internet connection and all the development tools we need! We can produce the next incarnation of Windows without leaving this room!

A bunch of VPs are going to write Windows 2000?

It's well timed for armageddon.

Oh no. This is Waco all over again.

We're almost at the loading bay. Stay quiet...

AAAAAAAHHHH! HALT!

SPROING!

It's just a cardboard model. Fake security.

Jeez, that's a first for Microsoft.

POKE POKE

That DOJ agent is going to expect us to assault that boardroom any minute now. Where's Pitr gone to?

He said something about having to save the world from the digital version of a "plague and pestilence."

Microsoft
LOADING ZONE "D"

Look buddy, you need to get out of the way. I have deliveries to make!

NYET! The evil stops here!

"This is where you will go today"

I don't think Pitr thought this through properly. How are we going to storm the boardroom with no weapons?

The Dust Puppy's gone to get the weapons Pitr left in the van.

Weapons? They're Snurf Guns! How can suction-cup darts scare anyone?

Urrrrrrrffff....

SCRAAAPE

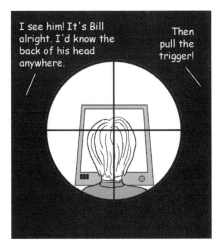

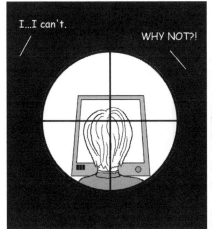

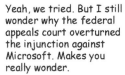

Mr. Moff, this is our company controller. Mr. Moff is a consultant.

Is there some deep, Jungian yet abnormally annoying reason why the two of you have to keep **smiling** at each other??!

I'm going back to work. I swear there is something terminally wrong with the two of you.

I suppose I can take comfort in the fact that **one** of you is going to have to stop smiling first.

You're messing with the best, rookie.

I'll stop smiling when the world comes to an end, and not a second sooner.

Chief, I don't like that consultant fellow. There's something very strange about him and he gives me the creeps. I don't recommend we hire him.

I just thought you should know.

You wouldn't have, perchance, stopped smiling first?

Hey, that has **nothing** to do with it!

So you're A.J., the company's creative guy. Let's work together and see what it is we can collectively spawn in the warm womb of personal satisfaction at the workplace.

We can take a detour through your superego, and fulfill your needs as an artist! Let go, young A.J., and we can blend the juices of our thoughts in a puree of creative genius!

Rejoice! Revel in your ability to empower the genius within you! Bring small toys to work and put them on your desk!

WAVE GESTURE

Would someone please get this guy away from me? He wants to blend my juices.

So Mike, let's see how I can help you with your duties as a system administrator. I understand you're having problems with some of the hardware.

Well, yes, kind of. We're getting a lot of traffic on one of our servers. The solution is to spread the load across the network.

Hmmm...

I suggest that you spread the load across the network instead. Let me know how it works out.

How the hell does he do that?

Well, hello there.

um...

Why is that thing smiling at me?

Disconcerting, isn't it?

He started it.

60

Tech support, Greg speaking.

Hello. Do I have to buy stamps to send e-mail?

No...no, m'am. You do not need to buy stamps to send e-mail.

Okay. Bye.

Another stupid question?

There's no such thing as a stupid question, only stupid people.

That's an interesting-looking book. "Managing an NT Server and Network."

You know Greg, I had almost given up on you and those stupid Linux servers. It's nice to see you're accepting the fact that NT servers are the only way to go for Internet service provision.

So have you read much of it?

Actually, I just use it to keep the lid down on my instant noodles.

I can't believe you actually **eat** that crud. It's going to kill you one day.

Hey c'mon. Instant noodles are full of nutrition.

It lists styrofoam and salt as ingredients. In that order.

That and a litre of Coke and I'm set for the day.

SSSTHFFFFFF

SSHHLUURRRP

Ahh, instant noodle broth. Nectar of the gods.

Which god, Cthulhu?

THE COMPUTER GEEK NUTRITION PYRAMID

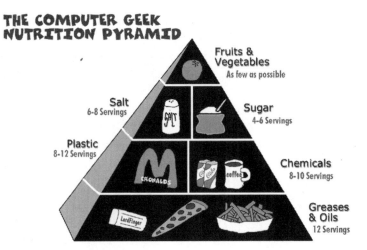

Fruits & Vegetables
As few as possible

Salt
6-8 Servings

Sugar
4-6 Servings

Plastic
8-12 Servings

Chemicals
8-10 Servings

Greases & Oils
12 Servings

Good God, all these heart disease and carcinogen warnings on the Web are terrifying. I'm going to have to cut out all the Cola I drink...

You do of course realize I can't let you do that.

No more greasy pizza before bed either.

63

Um, Pitr? What precisely are you doing right now?

Am in cnn.com's web server. Is shockink how truth is no beink reported.

For example, see. Headline sayink, "Ken Starr subpoenas Clinton in Lewinsky hearink." But they are hidink truth from public. I will now fix, make better.

"Ken Starr asks Clinton, 'How do I get some of that?'"

The dark side, she is seductive, da?

TAP TAP TAPPY

Lookink, there is more not-truths here. On Microsoft web site.

TAP TAP TAPPY

"In a move designed to broaden his management team to take advantage of future opportunities, Microsoft CEO Bill Gates today appointed Steven Ballmer president of Microsoft." Seems honest to me...

Wait a minute! I didn't order any of this! Thorns? Spikes?

Mr. Gates ordered it for you, Mr. Ballmer. The crucifix is still in the truck. Could you lend me a hand?

thoms 72 pcs

spikes 36 pcs

loincloth 2 pcs

DOJ not doink well against Microsoft. Am concerned they will lose steam. Must fix situation, da Stef?

I guess. What are you planning on doing?

Not beink worried. Pitr fix.

RAPPA TAPPA

Did you just make a change to Microsoft's web page?

Da. Now watchink the fireworks.

The Microsoft Web site said WHAT?!

I quote, "Hey Janet! Thpffffft!" What do you think it means Ms. Reno?

66

Is it just me or is it really quiet today?

It's not just you. I'm pretty bored.

I could always suspend a few hundred accounts and watch what happens.

Okay, but do it without rhyme or reason. AOL did that and **still** made bags of money.

TAP TAPPY

Microsoft spokesmen today announced that the company was filing a lawsuit against 20 state attorneys general for "unconstitutionally undermining the company's intellectual property rights."

Details of the suit were presented in chambers by a Microsoft lawyer. The final point covered by the suit stated that Internet Explorer has gained share on its own merits and not because the company exploited its operating system monopoly.

The dead silence that followed was broken by a loud burst of raucous laughter. The judge participated.

FRIENDLY the comic strip

Hello. I just heard a joke that I'd like to tell. When Mike told it, everyone laughed, so it's probably very funny.

A man is flying around in a hot air balloon. He suddenly realizes he's lost, so he reduces his altitude and approaches a man on the ground below. He shouts, "Excuse me, can you tell me where I am?"

The man below says, "Yes, you're in a hot air balloon, about thirty feet off the ground." To which the balloonist replies, "You must work in Information Technology." The man on the ground says, "Yes, I do. How did you know?"

"Well, everything you told me was technically correct, but it's no use to anyone." To which the man on the ground replied, "You must work in business." "Yes," said the balloonist, "How did you know?"

"Well, you don't know where you are, or where you're going, but you expect me to be able help. You're in the same position before we met, but now it's my fault."

It wasn't funny the first time either.

Wow, it's been a really long time since I played a good game of Quake. Time to kick some butt.

BAZING
BLAM
BLAM
SPLUTCH!

Stef, you've **never** played a good game of Quake.

How can anyone suck this bad?

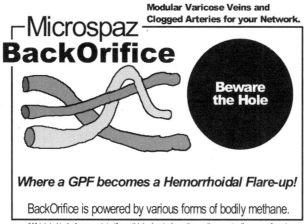

USER FRIENDLY the comic strip

Uh oh, Stef and Penelope are coming this way. I've had it now. They're... Hey, they're arm-in-arm.

Hey waitaminnit...

Hey, Penelope really **does** look like Ashley Judd.

She sure does.

I tell ya, I can't see a thing without my contacts. I sure wish I had them when I first saw her. **You** could've been having a great time instead of Stef.

C'est la vie. Better luck next time, Dude.

They'll never convict me.

Ah, you must be the CEO. My name is Mr. Padlock, and I'm the president of iCan't Internet. I'm here to buy your company from you.

I can't sell this company to you. If you acquire us, you'll axe all of my employees and replace our wonderful, homey workplace with a cold, impersonal corporate culture.

I'll give you two million in cash, three million in stocks, and a six-month membership at Nine Pines Golf Course.

You think I'm that easily bought? I want a **one-year** membership.

76

FRIENDLY — the comic strip

You must be that Stef fellow. Marketing and Corporate Sales, right? Well, we're going to see a lot of changes here.

For starters, we're going to cut back on hardware expenditures and give you a half million dollar per year travel and expense account.

Change is good.

Hi-tech businesses focus far too much attention on the technical staff these days. I intend to change that, and return the power to the **real** movers and shakers: the sales and marketing team.

As an initial step, we will make the workplace more comfortable and conducive to marketing executives. We now have a new dress code.

Behold.

You just go ahead and give me an excuse, and I'll rip you a new one.

Ah, Greg. Just the person I've been looking for. You look rather snappy in a tie and slacks I must admit. I think you techies have been missing out on corporate fashion for too long.

So now that you've been wearing a tie and shirt for a few days, what do you think of the dress code?

Oh, you're hilarious. For your information we haven't hanged anyone since our programmers failed to deliver product according to our marketing schedule.

79

FRIENDLY
the comic strip

Who are you phoning, sir?

I'm getting some help. We need to get NT installed.

Technical help?

Muscle, actually.

Microsoft Black Ops, how may I help you?

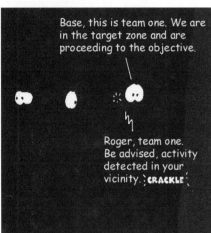

Base, this is team one. We are in the target zone and are proceeding to the objective.

Roger, team one. Be advised, activity detected in your vicinity. CRACKLE

KLIK

Uh Base, I have one really mad looking techie here, my team has abandoned the mission, and my gun doesn't work. Please advise.

Wait for the upgrade, Team Leader. Bye.

CLIK

TUNK
TUNK
TUNK

Hey Erwin. Watcha doing?

Talking to a server down in San Jose.

One of the iCan't NT servers?

Yup. Talking to him right now.

What's he saying?

"I'm in my happy place. I'm in my happy place. I'm in my happy place. REBOOT! HAHAHAH!"

That's verbatim.

84

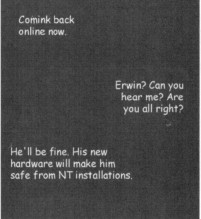

Look at it this way, Erwin. At least they can't install Windows NT on you the way you are.

I suppose you're right.

Why are you staring at me?

I have this urge to fill you with water and put goldfish in you.

Pitr, I just got word from San Jose. Our network has gone down nationwide.

Da. Am knowink this.

Of course there's an exception. It seems that the servers here are still up and running. Why do you think that is, Pitr?

Is because we are not runnink **crap** on our servers probably.

Unacceptable! We must have consistency! You will bring our servers down, just like all of the others!

Ah, Stef. With the servers down I can't send e-mail, and I have to get a document off to our bank in the Caymans. Could you fax it for me?

Of course, Mr. Padlock.

It's a two-hundred page document.

Oh. Well then you'll want to hand that off to Technical Support.

Ah ha! Is **that** what they do?

Oh yes. And they love the fact that the fax machine can't do a stack feed. Don't ever change that.

I need these pages faxed. I expect you to give this your prompt attention.

Okay.

They need to be sent to our bank in the Cayman Islands. I want them there immediately.

Yes, sir. Will do.

Are you wantink kerosene again?

I think I'll try battery acid this time.

My word, this is simply terrible. Our network is down, the bank hasn't received the signed orders, and I have a group of neurotics handling our servers. I feel like I only have a tenuous hold on reality...

Hello.

AAAAIIIEEEE!!!

Mikhail, you seeink Mr. Padlock runnink out door screamink?

Yep. That's one down, one to go.

I told Tufay that NT won't install on an iWhack. Not that he isn't trying...

INSTALL, DAMN YOU!

PAH-TOOEY!

iWhack

FRIENDLY
the comic strip

I wonder how the gang is doing back at Columbia Internet. Maybe I should give them a call.

Nah.

Hi Chief, it's Hillary. Mr. Padlock just ran screaming out the front door, and Tufay is away on stress leave. There's a real power vacuum over here right now.

The techs don't want to go back to work for the iCant crowd. Everything is running, and all of our accounts are right up to date. No debts.

Very good.

What is it exactly about all of this that concerns me?

Chief, just get your executive butt back here!

I suppose you heard about the San Jose office ordering new hardware to replace all of the machines that went down last week?

Da.

If they get that shipment of Pentium machines, they'll be able to bring the network back up.

Not to be worrying Mikhail. Pitr fix.

Don't Think.
1 pc

Don't Think.
1 pc

Don't Think.
1 pc

Don't Think.

Hey man, I just deliver them, okay?

I spoke to the Chief last night. He's on the next flight out of Tahiti. With any luck he'll be back by tomorrow.

The Chief's coming back?

Yes.

Guess that means I'm out of the running for CEO, huh?

We'd all follow you, but out of curiosity, not loyalty.

Chief, it's so nice to have you back with us. We really missed your management style and your sense of humor around here.

Oh, I just wanted to know one thing...

Why did you leave us with those bottom feeders?!?!

It's nice to see the Chief back here.

I suppose I have to agree, even if I will miss all my old perks.

Speaking of which, where is he today?

Dunno. He said something about "readying his mental space" for his return to management...

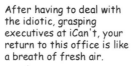

Pitr, Mike, this is Miranda. She's joining our company to help with system administration and tech support. Please make her feel welcome and show her the ropes.

Hey, guys. Nice to meet you.

We are havink problem with reality here, da?

What Pitr means is, how long have you been a woman?

USER FRIENDLY the comic strip

PIZZA

Portrasber 4

ROTO-ROUTER 800

This looks like a great company to work for. I can put all of my technical skills to use here with co-workers like these.

A female who groks UNIX? My universe is collapsing.

Am thinking she is EVIL.

I feel really threatened.

Man, she looks hot in jeans.

Pitr, thank you for taking time out of your day to help me get familiarized with the office.

And you are havink what education and trainink?

I have a Computer Science degree with a specialty in software engineering, I'm a certified network engineer, and I have six years of experience as a Unix sysadmin.

Da, I see.

Now payink attention, please. This is mouse. Click-click. Easy to use, da? Now you try...

FRIENDLY
the comic strip

So how're you doing so far, Miranda? Everyone treating you right? No problems?

Other than the ogling I've been getting from some of the guys, it's been fine.

The guys are ogling you? That is just **so** degrading. It's bad enough that our customers do it, but our co-workers should at least show a little respect.

I have to agree. I'm not just some bimbo with nice body parts. I have a mind, and an education. Why can't they see that first?

Well said.

Ladies.

Nice tush.

Sure, but he can't play Quake worth beans.

I can't take this much longer. Please get me out of here!

Relax, Erwin. Let's first see how well Quake runs on this.

BLAM!
BLAM!
BLAM!
SPLOTCH!

WIGGLE WIGGLE

Any luck?

No. This thing only has one mouse button. How am I supposed to switch weapons?

YOU SEE!!?? It's like being born with only one nipple!

97

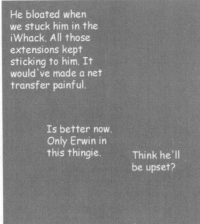

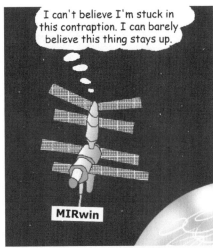

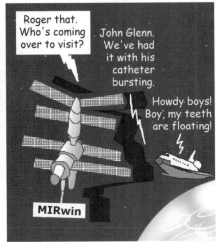

Microsoft announced today that their upcoming "Windows 2000" product would include a brand new feature.

Microsoft spokesman Barry Onimishon said "This feature will be the ultimate solution to the dreaded Blue Screen of Death that has plagued Windows for so long."

When asked what the new feature in the OS was, Mr. Onimishon smiled and replied, "The reset button of course. It's been used so much with our products we decided to officially incorporate it."

I'm beat. Sixteen-hour days were starting to catch up to me. But I had to do it -- the web site was an utter mess.

Too bad I'm on salary. I could have been raking in the bucks for the last few weeks.

Money isn't everything, A.J.

What idiot convinced you of that?

The Chief, at my last salary review.

Columbia Internet Tech Support.

Hi. What's the difference between the left and right mouse buttons?

TAP TAPPY

`ahem`

With years of education and experience on the front lines under my belt, I can safely say that the difference is that one is on the left, and one is on the right.

Hey! Are you making fun of me or something?

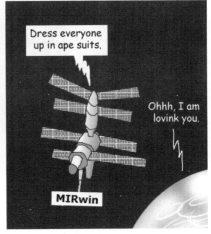

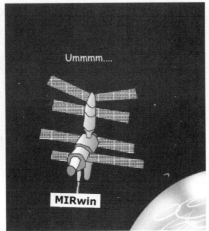

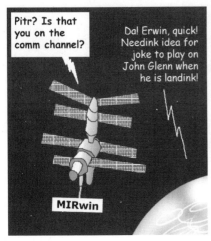

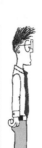

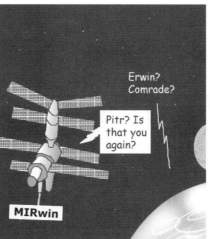

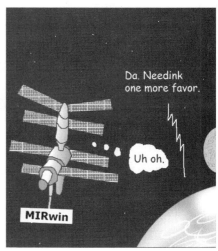

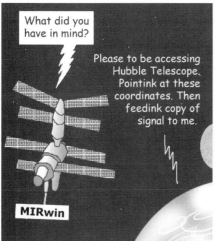

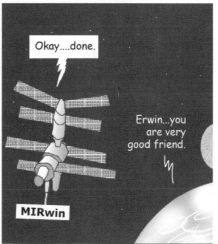

Greg, have you seen Pitr today?

He was with Miranda a little while ago.

Have you seen him since?

No, now that you mention it. I did see Miranda walking away with Pitr's prized collection of code libraries.

Now, for every e-mail address you spammed at AOL with my pictures, I'm deleting a random cluster from your code library backup disks.

MRRRRF!!!

TAPPITY TAPPY TAPPITY

Hmmm. Looks like the Microsoft trial isn't going so well for Bill.

Oh?

TAKK

Yeah. Something here about the Microsoft defense advising Bill Gates to use 'alternate tactics' when questioned.

Mr. Gates. Did you or others on behalf of Microsoft threaten to cut off support to Intel if Intel did not cooperate?

Ummm. These aren't the droids you're looking for.

ed with e Intel tives...

Thank God for this recess. That attorney is kicking my butt all over the courtroom. Mr. Gates this and Mr. Gates that...it's getting to me...

I suppose we'll have to.

I don't think I can handle much more of this, and my $1200-an-hour lawyers are hopeless. I need real help. **Come to me, my friend...**

Come to me, my friend...

Ohhh, am not feelink good. Why is stomach churnink?

gurgle Yes, my master...

BURP

ANATOMY OF AN ANTI-GEEK

Mind made for marketing, not ethics.

Suit by John Phillips of London. Cost: Enough money to buy a large array of quad-processor DEC Alphas.

Tie. 'Nuff said.

Mobile phone, for backstabbing and making deals, not just to fiddle with.

Legal documents. He understands them. 'Nuff said.

User Friendly the Comic Strip

http://www.userfriendly.org/

Look Greg, Mike and I aren't coming back down for a few days, and someone really needs to tell the Dust Puppy that his nemesis is loose again. Where is he anyway?

He said he was playing something really involving called 'Half-Life.'

Okay, time to ROCK!

A.J. and Mike are scared out of their wits, little guy. They tell me you know this Crud Puppy thing. Care to shed some light on the history you share with it?

Well. It is a long story...

...but every saga has a beginning.

You waited for days to use that line, didn't you.

144 PINTS
72 pcs

The little guy tells his story...

'A long time ago, in another incarnation, I stood on a desert world watching the many moons rise...'

'I had a quiet life, and what I really wanted was a life of adventure. I wanted to rebel against something Very Bad.'

Little did I realize how quickly my wish would come true...

Took you long enough to hit that rebel ship.

Sorry, sir. It's these Wing Commander reflexes.

Microsoft

I saw a bright flash in the sky and I knew that a battle was raging above my world...

Then I saw an escape pod falling out of the sky. Naturally, I ran over to investigate it...

My lord...the source code we're looking for is NOT in the main computer.

I finally managed to find my way to the escape pod. I knew my life was about to change from this point onward...

Little did I realize who I was going to get involved with...

Hey! You're a PENGUIN!

Let me guess. You're the galaxy's hairiest zoologist.

Linux

The stranger I met wasn't used to the heat and dryness of the planet Peedeepee. On our way to town we stopped so he could catch his breath.

Is it much further?

No. By the way, what's your name?

Linux

You mean, you don't know who I am?!

Actually, you do look familiar...

Linux

Aren't you that "Opus" guy?

Try again, herring-bait.

Linux

As we walked on, Tux the Penguin told me a fantastic story...

After all these years, the Evil Empire began to turn it's baleful gaze on to the good, clean power of Linux.

Oooooh.

They came after us with their troops. Our one strength was that our senior officers were more flexible than theirs...

How's that?

We can customize our colonels.

Uh-huh.

Lord Crud, we have located the escape pod.

:crackle:

Very good. Any evidence of whoever it was that stole the source code?

Tell him it's a duck with webbed as well as human feet. And it walks sideways.

No, my lord. Nothing obvious.

:crackle:

I have to admit it. The Rebellion is in trouble. We need help. And right now, I need help.

I know someone who'll help. In fact, he lives right around the corner.

Really? Who is it?

Tux, please meet Eric S. Raymond.

Dudes! May the Open Source be with you.

Eric agreed to go into town with us, so we continued on our way.

I could use your help in getting this data back to the Rebellion.

Why, what is it?

The source code to Windows 95.

Eric's thinking place

That's some bad ju-ju you're carrying there, bird.

That's nothing. I have their marketing plans too.

Grommet?

We left for Blackhead, the spaceport where Eric knew a pilot that could help us get to Rebellion HQ.

STEF'S FISH

Eric warned us that the cantina we stepped into was rife with the worst scum the galaxy had to offer.

LOO

Linux

Hi. I'm the VP of Acquisitions. You?

Careful lads! Don't let it touch you!

FRIENDLY
the comic strip

Guys, this is Lan Solaris. He says he's the best at everything in the sector.

And what exactly makes you such a hotshot?

I'm cocky and I know HTML.

We have data that we need to get to Rebellion HQ, and we need to get there quickly.

Imperial trouble, huh? It'll cost you extra.

All right. What do you want?

Something that everyone in the galaxy wants.

Fine. I'll do my best to get your name off AOL's snail mail list.

Then I'll see you at docking bay 1138 in two hours.

Your timing was perfect. I just finished an oil change. This is the fastest ship in the sector: the Millenium Bug.

Let's be on our way. We have an empire to thwart.

Did he say "Millenium Bug"?

I'm outta here...

I have a really bad feeling about this.

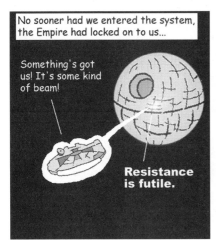

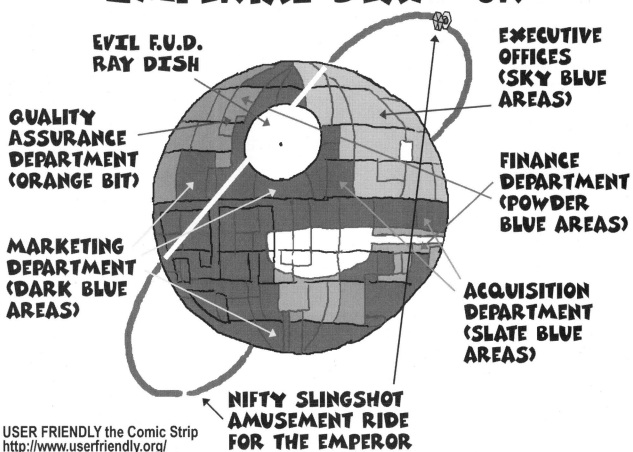

IMPERIAL DEATH OK

EVIL F.U.D. RAY DISH

QUALITY ASSURANCE DEPARTMENT (ORANGE BIT)

MARKETING DEPARTMENT (DARK BLUE AREAS)

EXECUTIVE OFFICES (SKY BLUE AREAS)

FINANCE DEPARTMENT (POWDER BLUE AREAS)

ACQUISITION DEPARTMENT (SLATE BLUE AREAS)

NIFTY SLINGSHOT AMUSEMENT RIDE FOR THE EMPEROR

USER FRIENDLY the Comic Strip
http://www.userfriendly.org/

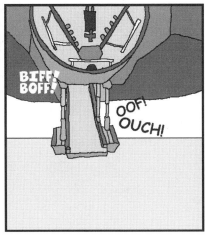

My old nemesis is aboard. I can sense his presence...

Yeah, sure. Weren't you the one who told the Emperor that 640K would be enough for anyone?

GAMEBOY

I find your lack of faith...disturbing.

I didn't mean it! 640K is plenty for Minesweeper!

ACQUISITION BEAM

PRISON

Okay guys. I'll go and turn off power to the acquisition beam, and you go rescue Lan.

Gotcha.

Mmmrff!!

Dudes.

Mrrf.

Is that what Lord Crud meant by 'downsizing'?

I **thought** that looked like Anthony and Garth.

CELL BLOCKS G-N-U

So do you have any idea where Lan might be kept? This is a huge prison level.

Rffm.

Hey! He looks familiar! Big hairy guy, looks like a wookie with a funny hat...

Mff mrr mr.

Hey, pipsqueaks, tell your wussy Emperor I'm **never** going to charge money for GNU!

Richard M. Stallman?!

120

DIRECTORY

Oh no! According to this directory, they've put Lan into the compactor!

Frmm mrrff!

COMPACTOR

Oh my, there he is...what's left of him, anyway.

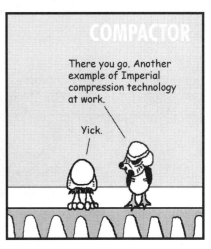

COMPACTOR

There you go. Another example of Imperial compression technology at work.

Yick.

The acquisition beam is finally off. Now we can leave this awful death orb...

And what mischief have you been up to, old man?

GNNK!

Ahh...you have learned to fear me.

Don't flatter yourself. I thought you were my wife.

Your powers have grown weak, old man.

Powers be damned. I'm going to beat the snot out of you with this hammer.

BZZZRRRNNN!

BZZNNTCHUNG! SPLUTCHBORTCH!

Ohh, that is so SICK!

Oh my god, they killed Eric!

GPF TSR
288 Pcs

121

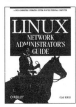

Linux

Using Samba

By Peter Kelly, Perry Donham & David Collier-Brown
1st Edition October 1999 (est.)
420 pages (est.), Includes CD-ROM
ISBN 1-56592-449-5

Samba turns a UNIX or Linux system into a file and print server for Microsoft Windows network clients. This complete guide to Samba administration covers basic 2.0 configuration, security, logging, and troubleshooting. Whether you're playing on one note or a full three-octave range, this book will help you maintain an efficient and secure server. Includes a CD-ROM of sources and ready-to-install binaries.

Learning Red Hat Linux

By Bill McCarty
1st Edition September 1999 (est.)
400 pages (est.), Includes CD-ROM
ISBN 1-56592-627-7

Learning Red Hat Linux will guide any new Linux user through the installation and use of the free operating system that is shaking up the world of commercial software. It demystifies Linux in terms familiar to Windows users and gives readers only what they need to start being successful users of this operating system.

MySQL & mSQL

By Randy Jay Yarger, George Reese & Tim King
1st Edition July 1999
506 pages, ISBN 1-56592-434-7

This book teaches you how to use MySQL and mSQL, two popular and robust database products that support key subsets of SQL on both Linux and UNIX systems. Anyone who knows basic C, Java, Perl, or Python can write a program to interact with a database, either as a stand-alone application or through a Web page. This book takes you through the whole process, from installation and configuration to programming interfaces and basic administration. Includes ample tutorial material.

Programming with Qt

By Matthias Kalle Dalheimer
1st Edition April 1999
384 pages, ISBN 1-56592-588-2

This indispensable guide teaches you how to take full advantage of Qt, a powerful, easy-to-use, cross-platform GUI toolkit, and guides you through the steps of writing your first Qt application. It describes all of the GUI elements in Qt, along with advice about when and how to use them. It also contains material on advanced topics like 2D transformations, drag-and-drop, and custom image file filters.

Open Sources: Voices from the Open Source Revolution

Edited by Chris DiBona, Sam Ockman & Mark Stone
1st Edition January 1999
280 pages, ISBN 1-56592-582-3

In Open Sources, leaders of Open Source come together in print for the first time to discuss the new vision of the software industry they have created, through essays that explain how the movement works, why it succeeds, and where it is going. A powerful vision from the movement's spiritual leaders, this book reveals the mysteries of how open development builds better software and how businesses can leverage freely available software for a competitive business advantage.

Programming with GNU Software

By Mike Loukides & Andy Oram
1st Edition December 1996
260 pages, Includes CD-ROM
ISBN 1-56592-112-7

This book and CD combination is a complete package for programmers who are new to UNIX or who would like to make better use of the system. The tools come from Cygnus Support, Inc., and Cyclic Software, companies that provide support for free software. Contents include GNU Emacs, gcc, C and C++ libraries, gdb, RCS, and make. The book provides an introduction to all these tools for a C programmer.

How to stay in touch with O'Reilly

1. Visit Our Award-Winning Web Site

http://www.oreilly.com/

★ "Top 100 Sites on the Web" —*PC Magazine*
★ "Top 5% Web sites" —*Point Communications*
★ "3-Star site" —*The McKinley Group*

Our Web site contains a library of comprehensive product information (including book excerpts and tables of contents), downloadable software, background articles, interviews with technology leaders, links to relevant sites, book cover art, and more. File us in your Bookmarks or Hotlist!

2. Join Our Email Mailing Lists

New Product Releases
To receive automatic email with brief descriptions of all new O'Reilly products as they are released, send email to:
listproc@online.oreilly.com
Put the following information in the first line of your message (*not* in the Subject field):
subscribe oreilly-news

O'Reilly Events
If you'd also like us to send information about trade show events, special promotions, and other O'Reilly events, send email to:
listproc@online.oreilly.com
Put the following information in the first line of your message (*not* in the Subject field):
subscribe oreilly-events

3. Get Examples from Our Books via FTP

There are two ways to access an archive of example files from our books:

Regular FTP
- ftp to:
  ftp.oreilly.com
  (login: anonymous
  password: your email address)
- Point your web browser to:
  ftp://ftp.oreilly.com/

FTPMAIL
- Send an email message to:
  ftpmail@online.oreilly.com
  (Write "help" in the message body)

4. Contact Us via Email

order@oreilly.com
To place a book or software order online. Good for North American and international customers.

subscriptions@oreilly.com
To place an order for any of our newsletters or periodicals.

books@oreilly.com
General questions about any of our books.

software@oreilly.com
For general questions and product information about our software. Check out O'Reilly Software Online at
http://software.oreilly.com/ for software and technical support information. Registered O'Reilly software users send your questions to: **website-support@oreilly.com**

cs@oreilly.com
For answers to problems regarding your order or our products.

booktech@oreilly.com
For book content technical questions or corrections.

proposals@oreilly.com
To submit new book or software proposals to our editors and product managers.

international@oreilly.com
For information about our international distributors or translation queries. For a list of our distributors outside of North America check out:
http://www.oreilly.com/www/order/country.html

O'Reilly & Associates, Inc.
101 Morris Street, Sebastopol, CA 95472 USA
TEL   707-829-0515 or 800-998-9938
          (6am to 5pm PST)
FAX   707-829-0104

International Distributors

UK, Europe, Middle East and Africa

(except France, Germany, Austria, Switzerland, Luxembourg, Liechtenstein, and Eastern Europe)

INQUIRIES
O'Reilly UK Limited
4 Castle Street
Farnham
Surrey, GU9 7HS
United Kingdom
Telephone: 44-1252-711776
Fax: 44-1252-734211
Email: josette@oreilly.com

ORDERS
Wiley Distribution Services Ltd.
1 Oldlands Way
Bognor Regis
West Sussex PO22 9SA
United Kingdom
Telephone: 44-1243-779777
Fax: 44-1243-820250
Email: cs-books@wiley.co.uk

France

ORDERS
GEODIF
61, Bd Saint-Germain
75240 Paris Cedex 05, France
Tel: 33-1-44-41-46-16 (French books)
Tel: 33-1-44-41-11-87 (English books)
Fax: 33-1-44-41-11-44
Email: distribution@eyrolles.com

INQUIRIES
Éditions O'Reilly
18 rue Séguier
75006 Paris, France
Tel: 33-1-40-51-52-30
Fax: 33-1-40-51-52-31
Email: france@editions-oreilly.fr

Germany, Switzerland, Austria, Eastern Europe, Luxembourg, and Liechtenstein

INQUIRIES & ORDERS
O'Reilly Verlag
Balthasarstr. 81
D-50670 Köln
Germany
Telephone: 49-221-973160-91
Fax: 49-221-973160-8
Email: anfragen@oreilly.de (inquiries)
Email: order@oreilly.de (orders)

Canada *(French language books)*

Les Éditions Flammarion ltée
375, Avenue Laurier Ouest
Montréal (Québec) H2V 2K3
Tel: 00-1-514-277-8807
Fax: 00-1-514-278-2085
Email: info@flammarion.qc.ca

Hong Kong

City Discount Subscription Service, Ltd.
Unit D, 3rd Floor, Yan's Tower
27 Wong Chuk Hang Road
Aberdeen, Hong Kong
Tel: 852-2580-3539
Fax: 852-2580-6463
Email: citydis@ppn.com.hk

Korea

Hanbit Media, Inc.
Sonyoung Bldg. 202
Yeksam-dong 736-36
Kangnam-ku
Seoul, Korea
Tel: 822-554-9610
Fax: 822-556-0363
Email: hant93@chollian.dacom.co.kr

Philippines

Mutual Books, Inc.
429-D Shaw Boulevard
Mandaluyong City, Metro
Manila, Philippines
Tel: 632-725-7538
Fax: 632-721-3056
Email: mbikikog@mnl.sequel.net

Taiwan

O'Reilly Taiwan
No. 3, Lane 131
Hang-Chow South Road
Section 1, Taipei, Taiwan
Tel: 886-2-23968990
Fax: 886-2-23968916
Email: taiwan@oreilly.com

China

O'Reilly Beijing
Room 2410
160, FuXingMenNeiDaJie
XiCheng District
Beijing, China PR 100031
Tel: 86-10-86631006
Fax: 86-10-86631007
Email: beijing@oreilly.com

India

Computer Bookshop (India) Pvt. Ltd.
190 Dr. D.N. Road, Fort
Bombay 400 001 India
Tel: 91-22-207-0989
Fax: 91-22-262-3551
Email: cbsbom@giasbm01.vsnl.net.in

Japan

O'Reilly Japan, Inc.
Kiyoshige Building 2F
12-Bancho, Sanei-cho
Shinjuku-ku
Tokyo 160-0008 Japan
Tel: 81-3-3356-5227
Fax: 81-3-3356-5261
Email: japan@oreilly.com

All Other Asian Countries

O'Reilly & Associates, Inc.
101 Morris Street
Sebastopol, CA 95472 USA
Tel: 707-829-0515
Fax: 707-829-0104
Email: order@oreilly.com

Australia

WoodsLane Pty., Ltd.
7/5 Vuko Place
Warriewood NSW 2102
Australia
Tel: 61-2-9970-5111
Fax: 61-2-9970-5002
Email: info@woodslane.com.au

New Zealand

Woodslane New Zealand, Ltd.
21 Cooks Street (P.O. Box 575)
Waganui, New Zealand
Tel: 64-6-347-6543
Fax: 64-6-345-4840
Email: info@woodslane.com.au

Latin America

McGraw-Hill Interamericana
Editores, S.A. de C.V.
Cedro No. 512
Col. Atlampa
06450, Mexico, D.F.
Tel: 52-5-547-6777
Fax: 52-5-547-3336
Email: mcgraw-hill@infosel.net.mx